CYPRUS

Jack Altman

GW00724579

J·P·M
PUBLICATIONS

CONTENTS

This Way Cyprus

For Starters...

...this isn't just another Greek island. First of all, although they share the language and Orthodox Christian religion, the Greek Cypriots have long given up the idea of identifying, let alone unifying, with Greece. Then, the Turkish Cypriots in the northern third of the island are even more assertive of the difference. In fact, the peoples of both communities give the distinct impression that when the governments have finished squabbling, they themselves will be very happy to make the divided island one whole, independent country. No, Cyprus is Cyprus, an altogether separate kettle of fish. Very good fish, too—try grilled red mullet, or squid marinated in olive oil and lemon.

Third largest in the Mediterranean, after Sicily and Sardinia, the island covers 9,250 sq km (3,570 sq miles) with an impressively wide variety of landscapes. The coastline alternates craggy coves and soaring cliffs with a fair sprinkling of sandy beaches. Inland, green and fertile plains of orange and lemon orchards and market gardens spread out between two ranges of hills and mountains.

The Troodos mountains extend southwest from the inland capital of Nicosia to the ports of Limassol and Paphos on the coast. To the northeast, the dramatic spine of the Kyrenia range thrusts into the knife-like Karpas Peninsula, pointing directly at the coasts of Syria and Turkey.

An arid brown in summer, the Mesaoria plain between the two mountain ranges offers a brilliant array of wild flowers in springtime. Sheep and goats share the sparser pastures. While choice vineyards and olive groves cling to the lower slopes or cover a flattened hilltop, higher up on the Troodos mountains, there's enough snow in winter for some decent skiing. After centuries of deforestation, pine, juniper, cypress and even valiantly nurtured groves of cedar once more characterize the Paphos and Limassol forests.

On a Troodos hillside, Greek Orthodox monasteries shelter behind rows of cypress-tree sentinels. A ruined fortress clinging to a Kyrenia mountain precipice

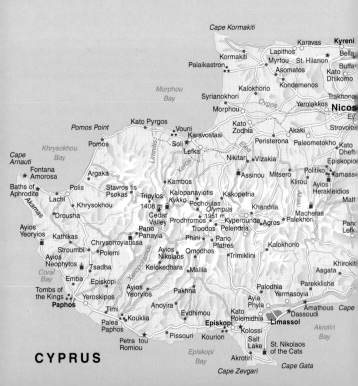

CYPRUS

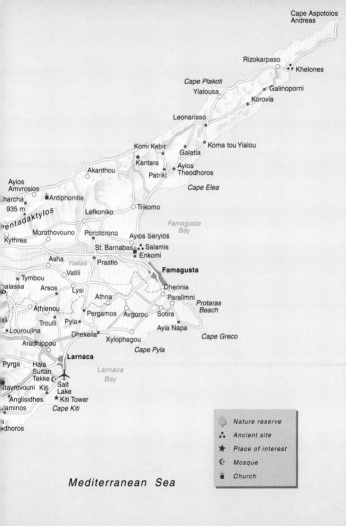

Cape Aspotolos
Andreas

Rizokarpaso
Khelones

Cape Plakoti
Yialousa
Galinoporni
Korovia

Leonarisso

Komi Kebir
Koma tou Yialou
Galatia
Akanthou
Kantara
Ayios
Patriki
Theodhoros

Ayios
Amvrosios
Cape Elea
Antiphonitis

harcha,
935 m
Lefkoniko
Trikomo

entadaktylos
Famagusta
Bay
Marathovouno
Peristerona
Ayios Seryios
Kythrea
St. Barnabas
Salamis
Asha
Yialias
Prastio
Enkomi

Tymbou
Vatili
Famagusta

halassa
Arsos
Lysi
Dherinia
Athna
Paralimni
Athienou
Pergamos
Protaras
Avgorou
Sotira
Beach
Troulli
Pyla
Ayia Napa
Louroujina
Dhekelia
Cape Greco
Aradhippou
Xylophagou
Cape Pyla

Pyrga
Larnaca
Hala
Sultan
Tekke
Larnaca
Bay
Stavrovouni
Kiti
Salt
Lake
Anglisidhes
Kiti Tower
laminos
Cape Kiti

dhoros

Mediterranean Sea

	Nature reserve
	Ancient site
★	Place of interest
☾	Mosque
👁	Church

reminds us of the passage of medieval Crusaders. In the coastal plains, more ancient settlers have left traces of their presence with ruins of Greek temples or Roman theatres.

As still expressed in the cuisine and the costume of folklore, the ethnic tradition is equally complex. Dominating the silhouette of towns and villages, the cluster of domes of an Orthodox church and the minaret of a mosque mark the island's dual identity. At the centre of the island, in the 800-year-old capital of Nicosia now divided by a wall patrolled by the United Nations, religious landmarks of Cyprus's two ethnic groups are visible almost side by side on the skyline. Similar Christian and Islamic monuments are to be found in the southern port towns of Larnaca and Limassol or in Turkish-controlled Kyrenia and Famagusta, where mosques have been established in the Crusaders' Gothic churches.

The climate is healthy, good both for sunning at the beach or walking in the hills. Summers from June to September are hot but not uncomfortably humid, with temperatures ranging from an average low of 21°C (69°F) to an average high of 37°C (98°F). Autumn in October makes a cool, sudden break before the November rains arrive, lasting on and off till March. The winter thermometer hovers between 5°C (41°F) and 15°C (59°F). Spring, in April and May, is a heartwarming delight.

Making Things Work

With a disposition as pleasant and cheerful as their climate, the people in this most hospitable of islands offer a relaxed but well-organized welcome. Even when you've convinced the wags that Cyprus is not just a Greek island under good management, there are others who point to the monumental letter boxes, orange beacons at pedestrian crossings and the cars driving on the left and suggest that it's in fact a British island with sun. Indeed, many visitors assume that the easygoing, unpushy efficiency of the shopkeepers, hotel managers and taxi drivers is a relic of British colonial administration.

Those who know Cypriots better can testify that the people did not have to wait for the Brits to come in—and leave again—before getting down to work. Not that they turned up their noses at the British-pioneered network of highways, a superb asset both for local industry and for tourists travelling around the island by themselves.

In the old days, the Cypriots made their money from copper—which is just what the word

Palm trees on a sandy beach suggest that the shores of Africa are not so far away.

Cyprus originally meant. It also provides the colour in which the island is depicted on the national flag. Today, in addition to the lucrative tourist trade, valuable revenue is earned by wine and fruit exports and clothes manufacturing.

From time immemorial, foreigners have been attracted to the island's strategic location in the northeast corner of the Mediterranean. Among the first visitors were Phoenician pirates and traders (in ancient days, the distinction between the two was vague), then conquerors from all the great empires—Egyptian, Persian, Greek, Roman, Ottoman and British. Not forgetting the French Crusaders, Venetian and Genoese merchants who made frequent visits to these shores, it's easy to appreciate that the Cypriots have had plenty of opportunity to learn the noble art of hospitality.

The modern invaders are not seeking conquest, just a pleasant place to sit in the sun, a taverna terrace where they can sip a glass of the admirable local wine or anise-flavoured *ouzo,* an easy hillside to ramble across, a *bouzouki* band to dance to in the evening. And then they go away happy.

7

Flashback

Historical Beginnings

It all started with a barbecue. Earliest traces of human life on Cyprus were some carving and cooking tools found beside the charred bones of a pygmy hippopotamus. Uncovered in a cave on the south coast, they are dated to around 8500 BC. With no sign of dwellings, it is assumed that hunters stopped here for a meal and moved on.

Some 1,500 years later, the first recorded residents built solid beehive-style houses, both in the southern interior at Khirokitia and at the northeast point of the Karpas peninsula. Abundant wildlife in the forests and fertile farmland in the plains nurtured good-sized communities of 2,000 and more.

The people were already a hard-working lot. The copper mined in the Troodos mountains from 3500 BC made Cyprus an attractive trading partner for other Greek islands, Egypt and Asia. Craftsmen turned out

Paintings in the Byzantine tradition cover the walls of Archangel Michael's chapel near Galata.

much-appreciated pottery, while Cypriot opium turned on pharaohs and other potentates. By 1500 BC, fortifications protected the island's wealth from greedy invaders. Egypt was bought off with "gifts" of copper in exchange for a formal military alliance.

Greeks and Levantines

Around 1200 BC, while mighty men from the Peloponnese were making their name in the Trojan Wars of Homer's *Iliad,* other more peaceful types sailed on around the coast of Turkish Asia Minor to settle in Cyprus. They gave the island a distinctive Greek character, with a new impetus and style in architecture, ceramics, copper and other metal industries. City states sprang up at Paphos, Kourion (near modern Limassol) and Kition (now Larnaca), Salamis (near Famagusta) and Lapithos (west of Kyrenia). They dedicated their temples to Aphrodite, the love goddess born on the island's south coast, and her husband Hephaestos, god of metalworkers.

After earthquakes ravaged the south in the 9th century BC,

Phoenicians from Syria introduced the Levantine component
of the Cypriot identity, notably
in their rebuilding of Kition.
Their sanctuaries, similar to the
temple built for King Solomon in
Jerusalem, were dedicated to
Astarte, fertility goddess and
counterpart to Aphrodite. Treasure in tombs at Salamis showed
that Cypriots happily combined
the Phoenicians' Oriental taste
for luxurious jewels with the
more sober Greek style of burial.

In the 6th century BC, Persian
invaders annexed Cyprus to their
empire as a kingpin in their fight
with Greece for control of the
eastern Mediterranean. Cyprus
sided with neighbouring Greek
islands in an abortive rebellion
in 499. The Persians backed Phoenician exploitation of the copper
mines, while King Evagoras of
Salamis formed an alliance of the
island's Greek forces with the
support of Athens.

In this golden age of Pericles,
Athenian émigrés introduced classical sculptural styles both in local Cypriot bronze and in imported marble. The island's dual
identity became increasingly apparent with the Persians' influence in highly ornate jewellery
and in monumental fortifications
built during the armed conflicts.

Alexander the Great put an
end to Persian ascendancy in 333
BC. His generals imposed Greek
administration and fought in the
island after his death for succes-
sion to the empire. The city kingdoms were devastated in a long
series of battles and sieges until
294 BC, when the triumphant
Ptolemies of Egypt annexed Cyprus for the next 250 years.

Under the Romans

Recognizing the island's strategic importance, Rome took it
over on the pretext that Cyprus-
based pirates were being en-
couraged to attack Roman ships.
On a whim, Julius Caesar gave
Cyprus back to the last of the
Ptolemies, his lady Cleopatra,

1

THE BEST VIEW There is just one place from
which you can see the length and breadth of Cyprus: the
summit of **Mount Olympus**, 1,951 m (6,401 ft), highest
point on the island. Reluctant ramblers will be delighted
to learn they can drive all the way to the top on an asphalted
road. The view is spectacular—if you turn your back on
the military radar installation.

in 48 BC. After her death, Augustus retrieved it for Rome, in whose hands it remained for the next 300 years.

All would have been quiet but for the Christians and Jews. The Jews had been invited to Cyprus by Augustus's man, King Herod of Judaea, to exploit the copper mines. In AD 45, the apostle Paul came from Syria to preach the Christian gospel with Cypriot-born Barnabas. Driven out of the synagogues of Salamis, they moved on to Paphos where another recalcitrant Jew was struck blind for not letting them meet the Roman proconsul. This demonstration, the New Testament tells us, was enough to make a believer of the proconsul, "astonished at the doctrine of the Lord". In AD 116, Jewish insurrection against oppressors in Libya and Egypt spread to Cyprus. Lucius Quietus brought in an army from Libya to quell the revolt, wiping out soldiers and civilians alike.

Byzantium versus Islam

In face of a preference for the jollier deities of love and wine, Aphrodite and Dionysus, Christianity did not gain a hold on the island until the Roman emperors themselves were converted in the 4th century. In 327, Helena, Christian mother of Emperor Constantine, brought a piece of the True Cross to the island, founding the illustrious Stavrovouni monastery where previously there had been a temple to Aphrodite.

The Archbishop of Cyprus accepted the titular leadership—and military protection—of the Byzantine emperor but was sole arbiter of the island's church affairs. In 478, he bought his authority by giving Emperor Zeno the original manuscript of Matthew's gospel, unearthed in the Salamis tomb of Barnabas, Paul's companion.

Weakened by war with Persia, the Byzantine Empire could not stop an Arab invasion of Cyprus in 649. Arab troops landing from a fleet of 1,500 ships destroyed Salamis, and only reports of the imminent arrival of a Byzantine fleet stopped them occupying the whole island. But they returned four years later with a 12,000-strong garrison to defend Muslim settlers, henceforth sharing the island with the Christians.

Byzantine and Muslim rulers signed a mutual non-aggression pact for Cyprus—and its tax revenues. Apart from Paphos, Muslim villages were located in the eastern half of the island. Despite occasional offshore skirmishes between Byzantine and Muslim navies, civilian relations between the two Cypriot communities were more peaceful 11 than modern propaganda admits. In 965, Byzantine forces defeated the Muslim Caliphate's Egyptian fleet to take sole control of the island.

Crusaders—Christian and Commercial

Pilgrimages to the perilous Holy Land depended on the Byzantine governor in Cyprus for protection en route. In 1097, when the Ottoman Turks endangered Jerusalem's links with Constantinople, Crusaders stopped in Cyprus for food supplies. Later, routed Muslim commanders also sought safety there.

With the imperial capital cut off from the island by the Turks, a usurping Byzantine prince, Isaac Comnenus, proclaimed himself "Emperor of Cyprus" in 1176. His brutal tyranny was ended by the Crusader army of Richard the Lion-Heart, but the English king promptly emptied the island treasury for his expedition. He handed Cyprus over to a Frenchman, Guy de Lusignan, who imposed French-style feudal rule—with an architecture to match. Splendid mountaintop castles at Kantara, Buffavento and St Hilarion became models for fortresses back in western Europe. Similarly Gothic were the cathedral in the new inland capital of Nicosia (later converted to Selimiye Mosque),

Bellapais Abbey (near Kyrenia) and Famagusta cathedral (now a mosque). Catholicism became the official religion, though Orthodox priests still wielded considerable spiritual and local political power.

Crusades were good for business. Famagusta became celebrated for its opulent lifestyle. In the 14th century, Venetian and Genoese merchants literally battled for control of the trade. When their men were roughed up in port riots, the Genoese staged a punitive raid throughout the island and seized the port of Famagusta. Lusignan kings looked on helplessly until 1464 when James II paid the Sultan of Egypt a ruinous sum to drive out the Genoese. James died and the Venetians ran the island through his Italian widow, Caterina Cornaro.

The Venetians' handsome profits whetted the appetite of the Ottoman Turks. In 1570, the Ottoman army bypassed Famagusta, which was heavily fortified, to take Cyprus via the south coast. They executed Nicosia's military commander and dispatched his head as an eloquent message to Captain Marcantonio Bragadino in Famagusta. For 10 months, the Venetian led an insanely heroic defence— 8,000 Greek-Cypriot and Italian troops opposing 200,000 Turks.

Empires may come and go, but the fishermen of Ayia Napa set sail every day, regardless.

By August 1, 1571, with only 400 survivors, Bragadino surrendered and was flayed alive.

Under the Turks

After bolstering the Muslim population with 20,000 Anatolian immigrants, the Ottoman Empire let Cyprus stagnate. Turkish officials were interested only in tax-gouging. Out of indolence rather than conviction, they proved more tolerant of the Greek Orthodox Church in Cyprus than did the Catholic rulers. By the 17th century, the Sultan favoured the archbishop over his own venal officials in representing the people—particularly in collecting their taxes. The day-to-day relations of the Greek Cypriots with the local administration were handled by the *dragoman,* a Turkish-speaking intermediary. The job made Hadjigeorgakis Kornessios the richest and most powerful Cypriot of the 19th century.

The island's Orthodox Church blotted its copybook during the 1821 Greek War of Independence by helping Greek ships with supplies. The archbishop and three bishops were summarily executed and churches plundered while Ottoman troops from Syria and Egypt carried out massacres throughout the island. But 13

Ottoman rule crumbled as Greek and Turkish Cypriots alike fled in droves from the crippling taxes and corruption.

And then the Brits

Cyprus suddenly regained its strategic importance. With Russia making threatening noises, Britain needed a military base from which to protect ships using the Suez Canal. An 1878 agreement let the British run Cyprus for the Sultan, who remained titular owner. When Britain occupied Egypt in 1882, its bases there diminished the island's military importance, but Britain found it convenient to continue handling Cypriot affairs—for the next 80 years. The Brits of the Colonial Office may have seemed a trifle paternalistic, but Cypriots found them more efficient and honest than what they had been used to. They appreciated the reformed legal system, new roads, hospitals and schools.

The Greek Cypriots were sure Britain would assist them in their quest for *enosis*—union with Greece. The Turkish Cypriots, 25 per cent of the population, were equally confident that the British would not betray their alliance with Turkey. But the Sultan, on the losing side in World War I, had to give up all claim to Cyprus in the Treaty of Lausanne in 1923.

Throughout the 1930s, the Greek Cypriots agitated for *enosis* in what was now a British Crown Colony. Troops from Egypt had to deal with riots in Nicosia. Rebellious Orthodox bishops were deported and all political parties banned. Nonetheless, when Greece sided with Britain against Germany in World War II, Cyprus provided 30,000 troops for the Allied cause—in exchange for the restoration of political parties for a Legislative Council.

Enosis or Partition?

Offered self-rule after the war, Greek Cypriots continued to press for union with Greece— 96 per cent in a 1950 plebiscite. Their spiritual and political leader was the fiery Makarios, just 37 when he was made Archbishop. From 1955, an armed campaign was led by a Greek Army officer, Cypriot-born George Grivas. Based in the Troodos mountains, his right-wing EOKA (Greek acronym for the National Organization of Cypriot Struggle) destroyed public buildings and assassinated leftist Greek Cypriot opponents. Suspecting the archbishop's tacit support, the British banished Makarios in 1956 to the Seychelles and later to Athens.

Turkish Cypriots in turn rioted in 1958, demanding the island be partitioned rather than united with Greece. *Enosis* was seen as a danger to Muslim rights and to Turkish security in the Eastern Mediterranean.

With Turkey, Greece and Britain as co-sponsors, *enosis* and partition were both dumped in favour of an independent republic, proclaimed on August 16, 1960. Makarios was its first president and Turkish Cypriot Fazil Kuchuk, vice-president. Britain came out of the negotiations with two military bases on the south coast.

Independence, then Partition

The fragile balance of power between Greek and Turkish Cypriots proved unworkable. The constitution divided jobs in government, parliament and civil service along "ethnic" lines— seven Greek Cypriots to three Turkish Cypriots with a population ratio actually eight to two. Despite dual municipal councils in major towns, the Muslims felt disadvantaged. After communal fighting in Nicosia, a United Nations force came in 1964 to separate the belligerents behind a "Green Line" through the capital. The soldiers—and the dividing wall—are still there.

An uneasy stand-off with Turkish and Greek military protection of their communities ended in 1974. Trying to ram through *enosis,* the colonels' junta ruling Greece staged a coup d'état against the recalcitrant Makarios. From the safety of New York, the archbishop was able to arouse U.N. support and return as president (until his death in 1977).

But three weeks after the coup, Turkey had responded by invading Cyprus and imposing partition. Amid now familiar scenes of "ethnic cleansing", some 170,000 Greek Cypriots had to flee south and 30,000 Turkish-Cypriots migrated north. The "Turkish Republic of Northern Cyprus" established in 1983 (which only Turkey recognizes) covers 37 per cent of the island, most importantly northern Nicosia, Famagusta and Kyrenia. Repeating the population boost of the 16th century, 80,000 immigrants have been brought in from Turkish Anatolia. The north suffers economically in comparison with the Greek-Cypriot south, but mutual suspicion keeps the two sides from a solution which would guarantee minority rights in a unified republic.

When you talk to the people rather than the politicians and soldiers, it is clear they all want one Cyprus, no matter which side they live. It really is too nice a place to split in two.

On the Scene

Our sightseeing section divides the Greek-Cypriot part of the island into five areas, starting with the capital, Nicosia. Then, from west to east, lazy Paphos, with side trips up to the mountain monasteries and Akamas peninsula; the lively port town of Limassol and nearby historic sites; the pleasant resort of Larnaca and the beaches around Ayia Napa and Cape Greco; the Troodos Mountains to cool off amid the forests. Northern Cyprus is treated as one separate area for one or two day trips from Nicosia to the coastal resort of Kyrenia, the Crusaders' mountaintop castles, Famagusta and ancient Greek Salamis.

ISLAND CAPITAL
Nicosia, Into the Hills

Northern Nicosia can be visited only via the single border crossing used for tours of the Turkish-occupied part of Cyprus (see p. 50).

Nicosia

At the hub of the island, the capital is Cyprus's only inland city (population 180,000, not including the northern sector). Quite apart from its varied shops, fine restaurants and lively entertainment, it offers fascinating testimony to the island's historic identity. Trace the long story from beautiful antiquities of the classical Greek era in the Cyprus Museum, via the Crusaders' churches, ramparts built by the Venetians, the mosques of the Ottoman Turks, to the sad make-shift modern border dividing Greek from Turkish Cypriots. The Green Line of partition runs right through the town, with a barrier of barbed wire, rusty oil barrels and a wall blocking streets that straddle the border.

The Ramparts

You enter the city's historic centre through massive 16th-century fortifications built in a wheel-like formation that measures 5 km (nearly 3 miles) in circumference. With their 11 great bastions and three towering gateways, they certainly look powerful enough, but their hasty construction by the Venetians did not suffice to resist the Turkish assault of 1570.

Some of the bastions today serve the more peaceful function of municipal offices. The moat is in part used for children's playgrounds, public gardens and parking lots.

Named after the seaport to which it led, Kyrenia Gate is in the Turkish-Cypriot sector of town, while Paphos Gate is on the border. But the most famous, once chief entrance to the city, is Famagusta Gate, a monumental tunnel-shaped building in its own right. Through tasteful restoration, it has been converted into a first-class cultural centre. With modern art exhibitions on the walls, the old stone barrel vaulting offers excellent acoustics for recitals of traditional or chamber music and jazz. Plays are performed in the adjoining moat.

Cyprus Museum

Just on the Greek-Cypriot side of the Green Line, near Paphos Gate, is the nation's principal collection of classical Greek and Roman antiquities. The gold and silver jewellery, ceramics, sculptures in bronze, limestone and terracotta often reflect a distinctively Cypriot combination of sober Greek and sensual Asiatic styles. From Kition (near Larnaca), the bull-hunters painted on a blue faïence *rhyton* (Greek ritual anointing bowl, 13th century BC) are unmistakably Syrian. See the finds from the royal tombs at Salamis—a bed, ivory throne, sword, parts of the king's chariot and bones of his horses (8th century BC). Outstanding is the assembly of dozens of votive statuettes originally standing at

THE TWO BEST RAMPARTS In the days of cannonballs and boiling oil, a town's ramparts served, or so it was hoped, to keep the enemy out. The Venetians' massive fortifications in **Nicosia** and **Famagusta** failed to stop the Turks, but today they provide pleasant recreational areas, parks and cultural centres. With agreeable promenades offering panoramic views of the rooftops, each is a good place for starting or finishing your visit to the town itself.

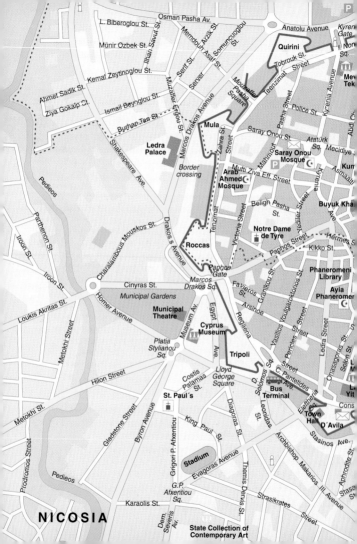

NICOSIA

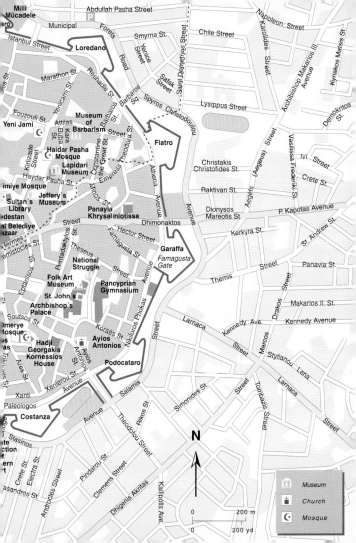

an open-air shrine—bull-masked priests, soldiers, chariots, bulls, sphinxes and minotaurs (Ayia Irini, 6th century BC). The best of the sculpture is a bronze of Roman emperor Septimius Severus (c. AD 200) holding forth as an orator.

The Old Neighbourhoods

Old Nicosia starts at Eleftheria (Liberty) Square, with its quaint colonnaded town hall and main post office. Inside the city ramparts, the busiest shopping area is along Ledra Street with food stalls and cafés for refreshment in the tangle of narrow alleys on either side.

Off to the right, Laiki Yitonia, which literally means "Popular Neighbourhood", is a lovingly restored and in some cases newly constructed quarter of traditional buildings—craftsmen's workshops and galleries, boutiques, tavernas. At the heart of it all, the Cyprus Tourist Office offers guided tours.

In a handsome neoclassical house on Hippocrates Street, the Leventis Museum presents the town's history with colourful costumes and household goods. The exhibit starts in modern times and goes back through Nicosia's British, Turkish, Venetian, Crusader and Byzantine rulers to its ancient Greek beginnings.

WHAT'S IN A NAME?

In the Middle Ages, the Greeks called the town "Lefkosia", distorted by French Crusaders into "Nicosie" and by the English into "Nicosia". To the Turks, it is "Lefkosha". According to historians, the name is derived either from Leukon, son of Egypt's Ptolemy I, founder of the city in the 4th century BC, or from the Greek word *lefki*, meaning "poplar".

Konak Mansion (18 Patriarch Gregorios Street) is the opulent home of Hadjigeorgakis Kornessios, Cyprus's most illustrious *dragoman*. To appreciate the profits to be made from such a post, take a good look at the ornate Gothic entrance, balconies, elaborate staircase and luxurious interiors.

Omerye Mosque is the main Islamic monument in the Greek-Cypriot half of Nicosia, used by the sector's Arab students and a few other Muslim residents. A soaring minaret distinguishes what was once the church of St Mary's, part of an Augustinian monastery converted by the Turks in the 16th century. For a view across the whole city and to the Kyrenia Mountains, the mosque's guardians will let you climb up the minaret to where the muezzin calls the faithful to prayer.

The Byzantine Heritage

The finest icons of the island's Orthodox churches have been assembled at the Byzantine Museum in a wing of the Archbishop's Palace. The oldest of these beautifully displayed jewels of Byzantine art is a touchingly simple 9th-century painting of the Virgin Mary. From the 12th-century heyday for Cypriot icons, many of them rescued from the obscurity of refuges in the Troodos and Kyrenia Mountains, you can see a splendid *Benediction of Jesus* and a poignant *Mary and Child.* The upper floor is devoted to later European painting, notably portraits of Greek islanders and their Turkish rulers. Some of the works are attributed to French masters Courbet and Delacroix, who gave their support to the fight for Greek independence.

The larger, residential part of the Archbishop's Palace is a modern structure modelled on a Venetian *palazzo.* It is closed to the public, but the town's tour guides like to point out that the island's great hero, Archbishop Makarios, slept there in monastic simplicity on a bed of iron.

Near the palace, the city's Orthodox cathedral, the church of Ayios Ioannis (St John), was built in 1665, more Gothic than Byzantine in style. Inside, you can trace the beginnings of Christianity in Cyprus in a series of frescoes from the 18th and 19th centuries. Among other episodes, they show St Paul and his disciple Barnabas on their mission of AD 45 and, four centuries later, the Archbishop of Cyprus receiving his special ecclesiastic privileges from the Byzantine emperor. The monastery building attached to the cathedral today houses a folklore museum showing traditional costumes, the looms on which they were woven, pottery, wood-carvings and the ancient tools of farming.

The Modern Town

Leading away from the ramparts, two busy thoroughfares, Archbishop Makarios and Evagoras avenues, are lined with shops, restaurants, hotels and airline offices. On the southern outskirts, a Handicrafts Centre on Athalassa Avenue employs potters, weavers, woodcarvers and leather craftsmen. They have in many cases been displaced from their homes in Northern Cyprus. Their wares, in general of much higher quality than the usual run of souvenirs, are for sale, but visitors are under no obligation to buy.

The remote location of Macheras Monastery made it a popular hideout for EOKA rebels fighting the British in the 1950s.

Into the Hills

For people staying overnight in Nicosia, here is a selection of several interesting excursions to be made into the surrounding hills.

Royal Tombs of Tamassos

The ancient city of Tamassos is situated near the hillside village of Politiko, some 20 km (12 miles) southwest of Nicosia. Tamassos is first mentioned in Homer's *Odyssey*, but the fabled copper mines which founded its wealth were initially exploited nearly 5,000 years ago. In the 1st century BC, King Herod leased them to Jewish entrepreneurs, who continued the mining until their revolt in AD 116. Apart from traces of a temple to Aphrodite, the archaeologists have uncovered tombs that probably belonged to rulers of the city kingdom in the 6th century BC. Beneath roofs sheltering them from the elements, flights of stairs and a narrow *dromos* (gallery) lead you to the burial chambers. Like many pharaonic tombs in Egypt, they are stone replicas of wooden houses, with imitation door bolts, window frames and roof beams. The sculpture and various other artefacts discovered here are now displayed in Nicosia's Cyprus Museum.

Ayios Herakleidios Monastery

Just outside Politiko, a monastery has been built to honour the memory of St Herakleidios, first bishop of Tamassos. Appointed by Barnabas for having guided him and Paul in their mission across the island, he was the first bishop in all Cyprus—until he was burned to death by infidels. The skull and hand bone which survived are kept in a bejewelled golden casket. All is sweetness now as the nuns who run the monastery spend their days gardening, and making and selling honey and marzipan.

Monastery of Macheras

Continuing southwest of Politiko, the road climbs through spectacular valleys and across dark forested ravines. This wild country around the monastery was the refuge of Cyprus's fierce EOKA forces led by Gregoris Afxentiou—killed there by British counter-insurgency troops in 1957. Standing 884 m (2,900 ft) up in the mountains, the medieval monastery was completely rebuilt after a fire in 1892. Its revered icon of the Virgin Mary survived the fire and still attracts hundreds of pilgrims every year.

Phikardou

The Macheras mountain road goes down past Gourri to this tiny village that is a living model of old Cypriot country life. The whole community has been declared an Ancient Monument and its unique multi-coloured ironstone houses painstakingly restored. Artists and writers find here a haven of peace, while visitors are shown over two of the most handsome mansions, with their furniture intact, a brandy still, wine press and weaver's loom. Have lunch at the local taverna.

Church of Asinou

Famous for its venerable frescoes, this 12th-century church, known also as Panayia Phorbiotissa, is beautifully situated on a hillside about 30 km (19 miles) west of Nicosia. Head past the old Nicosia airport to the town of Peristerona and follow the Asinou signposts. Amid lovely green wooded hills, the church is an unassuming little jewel in stone that changes with the sun from buff to ochre to amber. Its paintings cover 400 years of Byzantine art, from the 12th to the 16th centuries. In the dome of the narthex entrance, an *Enthroned Jesus* welcomes worshippers. In the *Last Judgement,* the wistful souls promised salvation in heaven do not look much happier than those damned to hell. Other scenes from Jesus's life and death are frescoed in the nave and side bays.

23

The charming fishing port at the western end of the island has become one of the country's most buoyant resorts. The pleasures to be had on its beaches and in the lively taverns fulfil its hedonistic mission as the ancient home of the goddess of love, Aphrodite. Cyprus's most celebrated deity was born (fully grown) on the coast at nearby Petra tou Romiou, and in classical antiquity Paphos became the centre of her cult.

You can visit the remains of Aphrodite's temple and see the rocks from which she emerged. Or take a trip up to the north coast to the pool in which the goddess bathed, and make this the starting point for a ramble along the pretty nature trails on the cliffs of the Akamas peninsula. Aphrodite's sanctuary at Paphos continued as a place of pilgrimage for the whole island until the 4th century AD—despite St Paul's conversion of the Roman proconsul here in the year 45.

Paphos

Earthquakes and successive invasions of Arabs, Crusaders, Genoese and Turks left Paphos (population 29,500) stagnating for hundreds of years as an insalubrious backwater. It began its recovery as a fishing port in the late 19th century and cashed in on the south coast's tourist boom following the island's partition in 1974. Resort hotels have sprung up all over the Paphos region, out to Moulia east of the port and north to the sandy beaches of Coral Bay and Ayios Yeoryios. Facilities for water sports here are first class.

For a change of pace, we also recommend cooler excursions inland behind Paphos to the monasteries and colourful hospitable villages at the western end of the Troodos Mountains.

Like many a maritime community of Greek origin, Paphos divides into a lower town, *Kato Paphos,* around the harbour where most of the resort facilities are concentrated, and an upper town, the hilltop *Ktima,* where the municipality has its shops, market and schools.

Kato (Lower) Paphos

A promenade along the waterfront takes you past souvenir shops and seafood tavernas to the old harbour. Moored alongside the fishing vessels and private sailboats are motor launches for cruises around the port and

This petrified "Peeping Tom" has watched many a loving couple meeting at the spot where Aphrodite stepped ashore.

along the coast. Behind the port, archaeologists are constantly uncovering vestiges of the town's Greek, Roman, Early Christian and Byzantine inhabitants, the most famous being mosaics from 1,800-year-old Roman villas.

The Old Fort

For the past 2,000 years, the square fortification standing at the elbow of the harbour jetty has been built and destroyed and rebuilt again by the Romans, by French Crusaders, merchants of Venice and Genoa, and the Ottoman Turks. Last used as a salt warehouse by the British, it offers a superb view over the port.

Around St Paul's Pillar

Above the harbour, off Apostolos Pavlos Avenue, is the sprawling archaeological site of the town's ancient Christian edifices. They are grouped around a marble column said to be the pillar where St Paul was given 39 lashes for his subversive preaching. But that happened more than 300 years before the marble was imported. The pillar is in fact one of the columns of a 4th-century Christian basilica destroyed in the Arab invasion of 653. You can see Arabic graffiti on some of the other broken columns, as well as ornate Corinthian capitals and geometric and floral mosaic 25

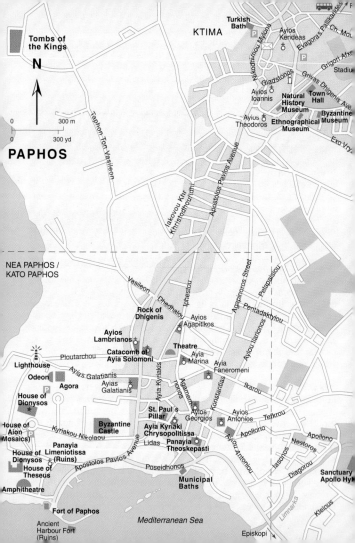

paving. One of the basilica's seven aisles is now occupied by the 15th-century Chrysopolitissa (or Ayia Kyriaki) church. It was transformed from the Latin to the Byzantine rite and is used today for Anglican and Catholic services. You can also make out the Gothic ruins of another church, built by the Lusignan French.

Byzantine Castle

"Byzantine" is a misnomer for what has now been identified by scholars as a French Crusader castle built in the late 12th century, some 30 years before its destruction by earthquake. Sheep now graze among the eloquent ruins west of Apostolos Pavlos Avenue, dubbed by the people of Paphos *Saranda Kolones,* for the 40 columns they counted strewn around the site. The fortifications were originally built on a rectangular plan, with eight bastions on a massive exterior wall protecting an inner four-towered keep.

Odeon

Northwest of the castle, a 14-tiered Roman theatre from the 2nd century AD has been rebuilt on its hillside, near a modern lighthouse, to seat 1,250 spectators for open-air festivities. The Odeon was originally part of the entertainment provided for patients at the ancient Paphos health spa.

Roman Mosaics

Paphos can justly claim to possess the island's most charming antiquities in its mosaics depicting wild animals, peasants, lovers, gods and goddesses. Further west along the road from the Byzantine Castle, these brightly coloured pavements decorated the floors of villas belonging to Roman patricians in the 3rd century AD. They were uncovered in the process of earth levelling for land development in 1962 and damaged in the 1974 Turkish bombardments, but they are now beautifully restored. The stone cubes used in the mosaics are naturally coloured.

Ongoing excavations are constantly revealing new mosaics, but three houses are presently open to the public, each named after a principal mythological character portrayed in the pavements. The House of Dionysus is devoted principally to the god of wine, riding in a chariot drawn by panthers and trying to stop a nymph drinking too much wine from her bowl. Other scenes show Phaedra throwing an incestuous glance at Hippolytus, lovers Pyramus and Thisbe (famous from *A Midsummer Night's Dream*), and a tiger, bear and leopard prowling around the atrium. The mosaic of the Villa of Theseus depicts the hero slaying the Minotaur in the

27

labyrinth at Knossos. In the House of Aion, a mosaic shows in five scenes a beauty contest in which the god of eternity, Aion, chooses Cassiopeia over a group of crestfallen water nymphs— much prettier to the modern eye.

Tombs of the Kings

The necropolis lies north of the city off the road leading to the resort hotels and villas of Coral Bay. From the 3rd century BC to the 3rd century AD, the Greeks and Romans of ancient Paphos buried their dead in underground chambers cut from the russet-coloured coastal rock. As an outpost of the Ptolemaic empire in Egypt, the tombs follow the pharaonic custom of reproducing for the afterlife models of the dwellings of the living: rooms are grouped in one or two storeys around an atrium or courtyard of Doric columns crowned by intricate stone carving. Though at the time Paphos had no kings to justify the tombs' present-day name, the impressive size and design of the burial chambers indicate their occupants were at least the town's most prominent citizens.

Ktima (Upper Town)

The people of modern Paphos have reserved for themselves a cheerful hilltop location high above the resort harbour. Public buildings are in bright neoclassical style and the bustling fruit and vegetable market is well worth a visit if you're planning a picnic.

Take a look at the District Museum of Antiquities on Grivas Dhigenis Avenue. The oriental design of the ancient jewellery, glassware and ceramics underlines the island's strong attachment to the Levant as much as to Greece. A sensual bust of Isis, Egypt's goddess of fertility,

3

THE THREE BEST BEACHES Depends what you want. On the island's west coast, family bathing is popular at **Coral Bay**, just north of Paphos, where the peculiarity is the pink sand formed by granulated coral. For a quieter swim away from the madding crowd, try the other end of the island, out on its southeast tip where **Cape Greco** offers sandy coves or spectacular rocky creeks great for snorkelling. The finest sands for building a really good Crusaders' castle are to be found at the increasingly popular **Protaras**, just north of Ayia Napa.

makes a seductive counterpart to the cooler statues of Diana the Huntress, Dionysos and Aphrodite.

The George Eliades Ethnological Museum on Exo Vrysis St displays in the professor's 19th-century home his private collection of Cypriot folk art, Greek and Roman antiquities and prehistoric fossils from the region. In his own garden, he has excavated a series of rock-cut burial chambers over 2,000 years old.

Along the Coast

Using Paphos as your base, you can make easy excursions east along the Limassol coastal highway in search of Aphrodite.

Yeroskipos

In recent years, this pretty little village has practically become an eastern suburb of Paphos. The name meaning "Holy Garden" dates back to its days as a resting place for Paphos pilgrims heading for the sanctuary of Aphrodite. It is renowned for its delicious Turkish Delight, but in these troubled times you're better off using the Greek word, *loukoumia*. Visit the town's charming five-domed Ayia Paraskevi church, built in the 11th century. Its treasures include a 15th-century icon venerated for the Virgin Mary and Child depicted on one side and Crucifixion on the other. The church murals date from the same period.

Nearby, an imposing wooden-balconied 18th-century house has been restored to become a Folklore Museum. It belonged to Britain's Cypriot-born consular agent, locally as influential—and prosperous—as the Greek Cypriots' *dragoman* in Nicosia. The exhibits include traditional furniture and farm implements. Taste some of the locally made carob honey.

ALL YOU NEED IS LOVE

Remember Botticelli's famous painting of the birth of Aphrodite (Venus to the Romans) floating ashore on a scallop shell? Well, it happened just down the road from Paphos. Here is how the town was founded: everybody who set eyes on the divine Aphrodite fell in love with her, Pygmalion no exception. To console himself after she spurned his advances, the legendary king of Cyprus carved an ivory statue of her for his bed—no inflatable dolls in those days. The goddess took pity on him, breathed her own life into the statue and bore him a child, named Paphos. Paphos begat Cinyras, who named his new royal city after his parent—the child of love.

29

Aphrodite's Sanctuary

Some 12 km (8 miles) east of Yeroskipos, signposts on the side road to Kouklia lead to the remains of what was once the island's greatest shrine, on a site originally known as Palea Paphos (Old Paphos). The sanctuary's spring rituals, the Mysteries, are mentioned by Homer, and the cult of the love goddess attracted worshippers from all over the Mediterranean. This was the beginning of Cyprus's lucrative tourist trade. Today, little is left of the temple itself and other holy places, though they are gradually being uncovered by painstaking excavation as archaeologists persuade neighbouring peasants to let them dig around the barns and farmyards where much of the sanctuary is still believed to be buried.

From the inner sanctum, the precious cone-shaped stone that symbolizes Aphrodite's life-enhancing powers is displayed with other ritual objects and ceramics in the nearby Palea Paphos Museum, housed in the Gothic Château de Covocle, a French Lusignan manor. The famous mosaic of *Leda and the Swan* has been transferred to the Archaeological Museum in Nicosia.

Petra tou Romiou

A short drive further east along the coastal highway is the spot where, as legend and local tour operators have decided, Aphrodite stepped ashore. The place was clearly chosen for its romantic arrangement of rocks out in the bay, some covered with shrubbery. Today it's a popular bathing spot for many a love goddess and her latest prey—snacks available at the café on the cliff above.

Excursions North

It takes a little more detailed planning to tackle the country roads, meandering across the western end of the Troodos Mountains to Chrysochou Bay on the north coast.

Ayios Neophytos

Some 10 km (6 miles) north of Paphos is a monastery picturesquely situated on the side of a hill surrounded by forest. It grew up around the refuge which St Neophytos, theologian and historian, carved himself from the rock in the 12th century. Opposite the monastery church, the *Englistra* (hermitage) consists of the saint's cell, chapel for meditation and sanctuary for the altar. Among the frescoes is a portrait of Neophytos himself in the company of archangels Gabriel and Michael. In the church are some admirable icons and frescoes of the 15th and 16th centuries.

Latchi

Just west of the busy little town of Polis, Latchi is the most popular of the Chrysochou Bay resorts on the north coast. It has pleasant beaches with good opportunities for water sports. For your shower at the end of the day, buy one of the natural sponges caught locally by Latchi's fishermen.

Akamas Peninsula

To stretch your legs from too much lazing around on the beach, head for the beautiful nature reserve of the Akamas peninsula west of Latchi. The wilderness has been celebrated over the centuries for its Baths of Aphrodite, a bubbling spring amid the trees where the ubiquitous deity came to cool off after one of her trysts. It is now the starting point for two delightful nature trails laid out by the Cyprus Forestry Department across the hills and along the cliffs (free maps from the tourist office). Among the flora to be found along the way: Calabrian pine, Phoenician juniper, carob, wild olive, fig, and strawberry trees (with deceptively bright red but very bitter berries); orchids, scarlet wild tulips, white and yellow rock rose, purple cyclamen. The fauna include 16 different species of butterfly, among them the orange cleopatra and twin-tailed pasha. Birdwatchers have 168 varieties to spot—bee eaters, blue rollers and the common black francolin. There are also many lovely creeks and secluded beaches for a quiet swim. If you don't feel like lugging along a picnic, there is a good seafood restaurant at the park headquarters.

Panayia Chrysorroyiatissa

This major monastery, whose name means Our Lady of the Golden Pomegranate, lies east of the Paphos-Polis highway via the town of Polemi. The mountain road passes through Pano Panayia, the village where Archbishop Makarios, first president of Cyprus, was born in 1913. Surrounded by vineyards and orchards, the hillside monastery was founded in 1152. The present buildings are mostly 18th- and 19th-century, extensively restored after World War II. Distinctive features are the triangular cloister and the church's intricately carved icon screen. The principal icon of the Virgin, encased in massive silver-gilt, is reputed for the succour it has offered to criminals and convicts seeking refuge in the monastery. The monks began making wine back in the 12th century, but have only recently resumed production, winning many international prizes for their light and cheerful whites. Try some.

SOUTH COAST
Limassol, Akrotiri Peninsula, Kourion

On a smaller, more intimate scale, the lusty, ebullient people of Limassol provide their town with an atmosphere comparable to many of the world's great port cities. They can justly claim to have the island's best restaurants. Their bars and nightclubs certainly offer the most exuberant entertainment after dark. During the pre-Lenten celebrations, their Mardi Gras carnival does with *bouzouki* music what New Orleans does with jazz.

Naturally enough, then, Limassol is the choice place for the island's wineries to base their production. The autumn wine festival is usually held in September, when the wine flows freely—and free of charge—with open-air concerts in the municipal park. If you're there at another time of year, you'll miss the festivities but you can at least visit a winery to see how the stuff is made.

The best excursions from Limassol are to the west of the city. The built-up area of the wineries gives way to sweet-smelling orchards of oranges and lemons along an avenue of cypress and eucalyptus trees that form a beautiful canopy of welcome shade.

Limassol

Limassol (population 136,000) was clearly of no great account in antiquity. The two classical city kingdoms were Amathus, still being excavated today east of the modern town, and Kourion to the west, a major Greco-Roman centre till it was flattened by an earthquake. As the place in between, Limassol was known in Greek as Lemesos, a variation of *Nemesos,* meaning nothing more than "place in between".

On his way to the Crusades to "save" Jerusalem, Richard the Lion-Heart made Limassol his port of call in 1191. After plundering the island's treasury for his military campaign, the English king was followed in Limassol by a series of other Crusaders, mostly of French origin—the Knights Templar, the Lusignans and the Knights of St John. Of the prosperity they brought the town, only one feudal castle remains. Other invaders destroyed more than they built, and earthquakes dealt with the rest. The British rebuilt the town by promoting the wine industry in the 19th century. Limassol is now the island's second-largest city after Nicosia. Expansion to its present size occurred with the

Lions' roars and gladiators' cries once disturbed the peace of the Roman theatre at Kourion.

population explosion in the last quarter of the 20th century, when refugees flowed in after the island's partition in 1974 and from Lebanon after its civil war the following year.

Limassol Castle

Set back behind the old fishing harbour, just a short walk from the tourist information office on the seafront, the town's one surviving feudal monument was built by French Crusaders in the 13th century. The fortress was expanded by the Venetians and occupied by the Turks after they conquered the island in 1571. In pretty surroundings of palm trees and other subtropical vegetation, the castle serves today as a museum of its era, tracing the island's history through weapons, stone carvings and pictures of churches and other buildings of the Middle Ages. It has been beautifully restored, particularly the Gothic Great Hall which looks too nice now for its eight impeccable white limestone cells to have actually served as a dungeon.

The iron balls and chains of the Crusaders' prisoners were probably manufactured by the ancestors of metal craftsmen still busy in workshops around the castle. In the alleyways, the 33 ancient skills are recycled today to bash out pots and pans in copper and tin.

Archaeological Museum

Housed in a modern building in Byron Street behind the Public Gardens, the museum provides a good showcase for the region's prehistoric finds and treasures dug up from Limassol's neighbouring Greek and Roman sites at Kourion and Amathus. (The sundial in the garden used to belong to Lord Kitchener.) Some of the island's oldest artefacts are on display—Stone Age tools and pottery from the nearby Akrotiri peninsula.

Sculpture, sarcophagi, terracotta statuettes, ceramics, jewellery and coins all testify to the rich culture of classical antiquity.

Outstanding are the torso of Zeus clasping an eagle (7th century BC), a lovely bust of Aphrodite and a huge statue of Bes, the Egyptian dwarf deity.

Museum of Folk Art

On Ayios Andreas, the town's principal shopping street, the museum illustrates the ageless village life of Cyprus with traditional costumes, richly embroidered textiles, jewellery and rustic woodcarving, with equal love and care applied to ornaments and everyday utensils.

Children are especially enchanted by the exhibit of a country bride's trousseau—her robes and heirlooms gathered together to be stored after the happy day in the splendidly carved wood chest.

4

THE FOUR BEST GRECO-ROMAN MONUMENTS
Earthquake and plundering invaders have devastated most of Cyprus's illustrious ancient treasures, but some choice sites remain. Paphos sets lovers a-dreaming with its **Sanctuary of Aphrodite**, while the main attraction near Nicosia is the intriguing group of royal tombs at **Tamassos**. West of Limassol, the Greek city kingdom of **Kourion** covers a sprawl that embraces villas with splendid mosaics, a Roman theatre and the exquisite temple ruin of Apollo Hylates. But the most prestigious of the island's archaeological sites is **Salamis**, near Famagusta in Northern Cyprus. The ancient city kingdom is famous for its college, theatre and public baths.

Yermasoyia

Immediately north of the main concentration of resort hotels, on a pleasant drive to the foothills of the Troodos mountains, the village constitutes Limassol's "gastronomic suburb". Amid delightful vine-covered gardens, the excellent tavernas specialize in locally caught seafood, along with freshwater fish from the nearby Yermasoyia reservoir. Amateur anglers who want to try their luck for the trout or carp should enquire at Limassol tourist information office about a licence from the Fisheries Department.

The Wineries

Limassol's major wine producers—Etko, Keo and Sodap—have their plants (combining winery, distillery and brewery) on the western outskirts of town, out along Franklin Roosevelt Avenue. Starting at a respectable 10 a.m., guided tours will show you the process of making and bottling Cyprus's wine, brandy and beer. With an option, but no obligation, to taste and buy.

Akrotiri Peninsula

Shaped like a blacksmith's anvil, the peninsula embraces a salt lake where birdwatchers can spot many a migratory waterfowl. In the winter months, until early spring, a touch of colour is added by pink flamingos. At the southern end of the lake, beyond the village of Akrotiri, are the Gothic remains of the Monastery of St Nicholas of the Cats (Ayios Nikolaos ton Gaton). In the earliest centuries of Christianity, the monks brought in a particularly brutal breed of cats to hunt down the vipers plaguing the island. Both the vipers and the vicious cats have disappeared. This was also the area where the burned remains of another animal, a pygmy hippopotamus, were found as testimony to the earliest known presence of human beings, probably hunters who had a picnic on the beach.

The strip of beach on the east side of the peninsula has been known as Lady's Mile ever since a British officer came here in the 19th century to exercise his favourite mare with a morning gallop. Today, part of the peninsula is off limits as a British military "Sovereign Base Area", negotiated in the 1960 treaty of independence (the other base is located at the west end of Larnaca Bay).

Kolossi Castle

This imposing four-square 15th-century castle keep towers over a pleasant stretch of greenery at the northern end of the Akrotiri peninsula. It used to serve as a massive fortified "head office" 35 from which the mostly French Knights of St John managed their vineyards and sugar plantation long after their crusading days in Jerusalem were over.

The main castle entrance was reached by a stone staircase and a small drawbridge on the east side. Over the doorway is the French royal *fleur de lys* emblem, part of the coat of arms of the knights' Grand Commander, Louis de Magne. But nowadays visitors enter by a door in the south wall. The interior is plain, on three floors, with two large, vaulted rooms on each. Up on the battlements, reached by a steep and much worn spiral staircase, share the lookout's view over the peninsula across to Episkopi Bay.

The Gothic building opposite the main castle keep once housed the sugar refinery. The sugar crop was lucrative, but the knights' pride and joy was a fruity red dessert wine which is still produced under the Commandaria label, after the formal name of their administrative headquarters at Kolossi.

Kourion

Remains of the ancient Greco-Roman city of Kourion (Curium to the Romans) extend across a series of separate archaeological sites at the northwest corner of the Akrotiri peninsula. To get your cultural bearings, you may

like first to visit the Kourion Museum in the village of Episkopi. It includes ceramics, terracotta statuettes, Greek sculptures and a Roman fountain in the form of a lion. Its most striking exhibit is a group of three human skeletons recently excavated from debris of the earthquake that destroyed Kourion in AD 365. Still in the positions in which they were found, a young man protects his wife and her baby.

The city of Kourion itself stands on a hill commanding a broad, sweeping view over Episkopi Bay. The town is believed to have been settled in the 13th century BC by immigrants from the Greek Peloponnese. Most of what survives is from the Roman and early Christian eras (guide maps to the site are on sale at the main entrance). The paving of a colonnaded portico has an amusing Roman mosaic of the 4th century AD depicting Achilles dressed as a girl in his abortive effort to dodge the draft for the Trojan Wars. Another finely coloured mosaic shows more manly warriors duelling in the House of the Gladiators.

The remains of an early Christian Cathedral shows it to have been of imposing size, supported by 24 granite columns. At the entrance, the devout were invited by a Greek inscription to "Make a vow and pay the Lord"—via the deacon's collection box.

See also the baptistery, with its cloakroom from which people stepped down to a sunken stone font in the form of a cross.

Roman Theatre

The theatre has been rebuilt at the edge of town, directly overlooking the sea. (From this spectacular position, criminals condemned to death were thrown over the precipice.)

When it was built in the 2nd century AD, the auditorium seated 3,500, but after hunting extravaganzas with untamed lions and tigers were introduced a century later, the front rows were, as you can still see, flattened to keep the spectators out of harm's way. The occasional open-air shows which are once again being staged here are usually more tranquil.

Villa of Eustolios

Immediately behind the theatre, this was clearly a handsome residence, perhaps even doubling as a hotel, since it also includes public baths and a small gymnasium. The floors are decorated with fine mosaics of animals, birds and Greek deities.

According to inscriptions, the patrician owner, who lived at the very end of the Roman era (early 5th century AD), paid homage to the old cult of Apollo as well as to the new religion of Jesus Christ.

Stadium

Kourion's sports stadium is situated a short distance west of the principal archaeological site on the other side of the road to Paphos. About 6,000 spectators could watch foot races on the U-shaped track; athletic disciplines included boxing, wrestling, discus and javelin-throwing.

Sanctuary of Apollo

Further along the highway, amid a small forest of pines and evergreen Mediterranean *maquis* heath, is the Sanctuary of Apollo Hylates (*Hylates* means "woodland"). This was a deer forest when the shrine was founded around the 8th century BC. The buildings you see now date from about AD 100. Just beyond the present guardian's hut, behind the Paphos Gate, are the pilgrims' hostels and various storehouses for their donations to the sanctuary.

A processional avenue led the pilgrims to the ceremonial stairway in front of the Temple of Apollo. Some of its elegant columns have now been reconstructed to the way they must have been before the earthquake of AD 365 toppled them all over. 37

LARNACA BAY

Larnaca, West of Larnaca, Ayia Napa,
Beaches and Villages

Since the 1974 partition closed
Nicosia's airport to civilians,
Larnaca has become Cyprus's
principal gateway for international traffic. The airport has
increased the city's overall prosperity, with the population practically doubling with refugees
from Famagusta to reach over
63,000. The harbour has become
a fast-developing port of call for
luxury cruise ships and ferries
from Lebanon, and modern
resort hotels have sprung up
along the beaches of Larnaca Bay
curving away from the city to the
east.

Larnaca

The city's fortunes have yo-yoed
up and down throughout history.
Phoenician merchants helped the
town prosper through copper
exports, but it suffered from their
alliance with the Persians against
the Greeks, ending in ruin after
Alexander's conquest. A brief
recovery to exploit the salt trade
from the local salt lake ended
with the Arab invasion in 647.
The town revived as a commercial port under the Crusaders,
slumbered again, then prospered
under Turkish domination. Over-
shadowed by the vigorous port

activity of Famagusta in the 19th
century, Larnaca has once more
flourished since the 1974 Turkish
occupation of the north.

After the Flood

Larnaca can claim to be one of
the island's oldest towns still in
existence. Archaeologists have
uncovered dwellings here dating
back nearly 4,000 years. The
town traces its historical beginnings to Mycenaean Greeks who,
in 1200 BC, established the city
kingdom of Kition, now buried
beneath the modern quarters of
northern Larnaca. Kittim, as it
was known to its Phoenician
settlers who took over in the 9th
century BC, is the name of Noah's
grandson in the Bible, and it is
to him that legend attributes the
town's foundation. Kition has
survived as the name of the
Orthodox Christian diocese.
President Makarios began his
ecclesiastical career as Bishop of
Kition.

In Town

The town's waterfront is devoted
mainly to pleasant cafés and
tavernas on one side of the promenade and on the other, a public
beach, marina for private sail-

The secluded rocky coves of Cape Greco are the place to go to escape the crowds.

boats and fishing harbour. To leisurely pedestrians, its whole length is popularly known as Palm Tree *(Foinikoudes)* Promenade, but its official names reflect historical allegiances: Athens Avenue at the north end, Ankara in the middle and Pyale Pasha as it passes the old Turkish quarter to the south.

Turkish Fort

Built in 1625, the bastion offers from its ramparts a good view of the harbour. A small medieval museum in the fort displays material from the archaeological site of ancient Kition and the Muslim shrine of Hala Sultan Tekke commemorating the Arab conquest in the 7th century. Stone tablets in Hebrew and Arabic testify to neighbourly relations that once existed here between Jewish and Muslim merchants. Opposite the fort beside a tiny cemetery with turbans on its headstones, the Grand Mosque was erected at the end of the 16th century. Only a handful of Arab merchants and students worship there today.

St Lazarus Church

Larnaca's patron saint, the man of Bethany whom Jesus raised from the tomb, is believed to have travelled to Cyprus to 39 escape the wrath of the Pharisees and become Bishop of Kition before dying his second death. An Orthodox church at the west end of Dionysou Street stands over the tomb of Lazarus, and its three-storied bell tower remains one of Larnaca's most important religious landmarks. In the wake of its many reconstructions, the church is a bizarre but not unattractive combination of Byzantine, Romanesque and Gothic styles. Inside, episodes from the life of Jesus are portrayed on an immense, carved icon screen. To the right of the entrance, an icon depicts one of the observers of the resurrection of Lazarus holding his nose at the smell of the revived corpse—"by this time he stinketh". The sarcophagus in the crypt, which no longer contains the saint's remains, may well be the origin of the town's modern name, *larnax* being the Greek for a stone coffin. In the neighbouring cemetery are the graves of British residents—diplomats, merchants and sailors—dating back several centuries.

Pierides Museum

A good collection of prehistoric, ancient Greek and Byzantine treasures are housed in the family home of Demetrios Pierides, Sweden's honorary consul in the 19th century. On Zeno Kitieos Street (near the tourist information office), the consul assembled a visual history of Cyprus from the Stone Age to his own era: pottery both in sculpted stone and in bright red glazed clay; terracotta figurines of Phoenician and classical Greek deities; five centuries of Roman glass; and traditional Cypriot household goods, furniture, costumes and textiles embroidered by Pierides' own family.

Larnaca District Museum

Regional antiquities are housed with a sculpture garden at the junction of Kimon and Kilkis streets. Highlights include findings from Stone Age Khirokitia, one of the island's earliest human settlements, and Early Bronze Age Kalavasos. From excavations at ancient Kition come limestone sculpture, alabaster vases, lanterns, carved ivory and other jewellery in both Egyptian and Greek style, and a great hoard of coins.

West of Larnaca

The Salt Lake lies southwest of Larnaca, on the way to the airport. Exploited since antiquity, the salt is farmed in July and August after the lake's waters, 3 m (10 ft) below sea level, have dried up. Like the wet mudflats on the Akrotiri peninsula near Limassol, the lake's waters in autumn, winter and early spring attract hundreds of migratory birds, including bright splashes of pink flamingos.

Hala Sultan Tekke

The shrine of the Prophet Mohammed's aunt, Umm Haram (known in Turkish as Hala Sultan), stands on the edge of the great Salt Lake. Its minaret and dome rise above a grove of cypresses and palm trees that in summer loom like a veritable oasis amid the desert of salt. The octagonal mosque was built by the Turks in the early 19th century as a monument to Umm Haram who was foster mother to Mohammed and accompanied the Arab troops invading Cyprus in 647. She is said to have fallen from her mule near the Salt Lake and broken her neck.

Her tomb here is now a major holy place for Muslim pilgrims. Take off your shoes before entering the shrine, which has bright green columns and, in the domed inner sanctuary, a dramatic stone structure marking Umm Haram's place of burial.

Panayia Angeloktistos

A short drive west of the Salt Lake, the village of Kiti boasts at its crossroads a remarkable medieval church of honey-coloured stone, whose name means "Built by Angels". The narthex (entrance hall) was orig-inally a Catholic family chapel. The most cherished treasure is a superb Byzantine mosaic, several hundred years older than the 11th-century domed edifice of which it is a part. In the apse beyond the uncommonly lofty nave, the Virgin Mary with the child Jesus is portrayed standing on a stool, flanked by archangels Gabriel and Michael. Since the plundering of comparable works in Northern Cyprus, this is probably the finest surviving mosaic on the island.

Khirokitia

Just off the Larnaca-Limassol motorway (Exit 14) you can see the remains of the oldest known village in Cyprus, dating back to 7000 BC and discovered in 1934.

The site excavated so far is divided into four "neighbourhoods" built on a steep hillside. (Statuettes, tools and jewellery found here among thousands of artefacts are now displayed at the Cyprus Museum in Nicosia.) Still visible are the circular stone foundations on which the clusters of beehive-shaped houses were built. Their walls would have been constructed with baked mud bricks, one dwelling just rebuilt on top of another as each collapsed. As revealed by skeletons found beneath the houses, a basement area served as a private cemetery for each family.

Lefkara

In a pretty location up in the Troodos foothills some 50 km (30 miles) west of Larnaca, the village that constitutes this historic centre of traditional embroidery divides into two ditricts, (lower) Kato Lefkara and (upper) Pano Lefkara. Women in the doorways of the narrow streets or hidden away in the shade of inner courtyards continue to practise their centuries-old craft known all over the island as *lefkaritika*. This is most often erroneously translated as "Lefkara lace". In the trade, as they say, it is more properly known as drawn-thread embroidery. The models used for the geometrically patterned open-work are more than 500 years old, but the basic material nowadays is Irish linen. Lefkara's silverware is also admired for its intricate workmanship. Before buying—the women's work is distributed through four local outlets—visit the Folk Art Museum in the old stone house of Patsalos to see the finest samples of *lefkaritika* and silverware. Or at least try the delicious local figs and home-made Turkish Delight, remembering to call it diplomatically *loukoumia*.

Stavrovouni

Midway between Lefkara and Larnaca, the venerable "Mountain of the Cross" monastery occupies a splendid hilltop site at the eastern end of the Troodos Mountains, at an altitude of 688 m (2,256 ft). Since antiquity, the spot has owed its sanctity to two women, but only men are allowed to visit it (they can also stay overnight). The shrine was originally dedicated to the goddess Aphrodite, even though it was forbidden to women. The monastery was founded in 327 by Helena, mother of Emperor Constantine. Devoutly protecting the piece of the True Cross she brought from Jerusalem, the monks observe the same strict regulations as those of Mount Athos in Greece. The tiny fragment said to come from the Cross is kept in the church in a 17th-century gold case. For unbelievers, a major attraction—apart from the monks' home-made cheese and honey—is the grand view south across rolling hills, over the Salt Lake to the Mediterranean, and all the way north beyond Nicosia to the fierce peaks of the Kyrenia Mountains.

Ayia Napa

For the tourist, one of the most spectacular results of Turkish occupation of the great neighbouring port of Famagusta has been the new focus on Ayia Napa, changing it from a sleepy

Lefkara's ancient crafts are passing to a new, mini-skirted generation.

little fishing village to the bustling centre of Cyprus's fastest-growing resort area. Thanks to the exceptionally fine sandy beaches that nobody thought to exploit before at this southeast tip of the island, hotels, holiday villas and tavernas have sprung up along the coast. The hinterland is a fertile market-gardening region providing the island with most of its potatoes and all the ingredients for a "Greek salad": tomatoes, cucumbers, onions and aubergines.

The town of Ayia Napa itself—it can no longer be called a village—climbs up a hillside behind the harbour, largely transformed now from fishing port to a marina for private sailing vessels.

Monastery of Ayia Napa

In the centre of town, a wall surrounds the delightful monastery church and cloisters, medieval in origin but completed by the Venetians in the 16th century. The wall built to protect the sanctuary from pirates now stands as a rampart against the surrounding cafés, souvenir shops, discotheques and tour agencies. Of the "Holy Forest" *(Ayia Napa)* after which the golden-stone monastery is named, only two 600-year-old sycamore trees remain, 43 below the chapel on the east side, plus a few new palm trees and cypresses. At the centre of the cloister is an octagonal marble fountain pouring forth its fresh water under a stone domed canopy. Built on a slope, the monastery's church is in part hewn from the subterranean bedrock. Notice finely carved Gothic detail such as a rose window above one of the doorways.

Marine Life Museum

Founded in 1992 and drawing on a private collection, Cyprus's first museum of its kind (it's not an aquarium) is a striking modern structure built around an open-air amphitheatre. A highlight is the display of fossils of sea life—fishes, sponges, ammonites, corals and molluscs—up to 220 million years old. They are shown in an imaginative reconstruction of the sea bed in the age of the dinosaurs. Specimens of the modern era, collected mainly from the waters around Cyprus and the Aegean Sea, include fish, shell fish and waterfowl, but also sea turtles shown in their natural habitat at egg-laying time.

Beaches and Villages

The southeast end of the island being very much a sanctuary for sun, sea and sand worshippers, people find it hard to leave the beach mattress that has become their prayer-mat. But you may be enticed away for a couple of hours to visit inland villages,

5

THE FIVE BEST MONASTERIES The independent spirit of Cyprus's Orthodox church gave rise to many important monasteries. Up in the Troodos Mountains is the most popular pilgrimage monastery of **Kykko**, where Archbishop Makarios was a novice. Perhaps the oldest is **Stavrovouni**, founded in 327 by Helena, mother of Emperor Constantine, near Larnaca. North of Paphos, the monks at **Panayia Chrysorroyiatissa** (Our Lady of the Golden Pomegranate) make their holy ends meet with the fine white wines produced from the monastery vineyard. From the architectural point of view, one of the most attractive is the monastery of **Ayia Napa** with its Gothic cloister as a peaceful refuge from the beach. In Northern Cyprus, see **Bellapais Abbey**, beautiful remains of the Augustinian monastery overlooking Kyrenia.

other resorts, more secluded beaches. At a point where, thanks to the Turkish presence in Famagusta, the territory of the Greek-Cypriot republic shrinks to a narrow coastal strip, you can also tour places that mark Cyprus's modern history.

Cape Greco

At the very tip of the island, on either side of the cape's lighthouse and radar station, the clear blue waters of the craggy coves and creeks are a snorkeller's paradise. But even non-swimming romantics come here to escape the madding crowd and enjoy the spectacular sunsets. Even better, they say, lovers awake with the sunrise.

Protaras

The fine golden and silver sands here and a little further south at Fig Tree Bay are ideal for family bathing. The resort hotels offer excellent facilities for water sports, and rent out equipment for use down at Cape Greco.

Paralimni

The whitewashed houses of this pleasant little town make an attractive setting for gourmet dinner excursions, both from Ayia Napa and Protaras. The tavernas prepare delicious fare from local seafood and the freshest of the region's vegetables.

Dherinia

Right on the frontier, the town is manned by UN troops guarding the road to Famagusta. Greek-Cypriot refugees make pilgrimages here to catch a glimpse of their old homes in the historic port from the observation decks on the north side of town.

Dhekelia

Unless invited in by a friend or relative stationed here, you can only drive around the outskirts of this second of Britain's two "Sovereign Base Areas" (the other being at Akrotiri, west of Limassol). It was used as a staging area for British forces participating in the Gulf War in 1991. The drive around Larnaca Bay offers a pretty view of the coast. Brits are amused by the street names evoking the glories of historic victories: Agincourt, Mandalay and Waterloo.

Pyla

Close to the border with Northern Cyprus, this ancient village is worth visiting for its fish tavernas, but also because it is the only place on the island where, despite the partition, Turkish and Greek Cypriots live side by side. In the centre of town, next to the medieval church of St Michael, a feudal tower remains from Pyla's days as a stronghold of French Crusaders.

TROODOS MOUNTAINS
Pano Platres, Troodos Town

The mountain range covering the centre of the island from Nicosia down to the southwest coast is where Cyprus cools off and gets its water for drinking and irrigation. All the main rivers rise in the Troodos highlands, and along the waterways are pretty villages, health spas, weekend resorts with mountain chalets and nature trails through the pine forests. Good overnight accommodation is available for those planning an early morning ramble. Around the town of Troodos, there is even enough snow in winter for visitors to indulge in a little skiing. For centuries, the mountains have provided spiritual refuge for monasteries and, more recently, hideouts for EOKA rebels against British colonial rule.

Today, holidaymakers on the coast can retreat to the heights for a refreshing day trip—most conveniently from Limassol, but also from Paphos or Nicosia.

Pano Platres
Not to be confused with little Kato (lower) Platres downhill to the west, Pano (upper) Platres is the main resort town of the Troodos region, 1,128 m (3,700 ft) up in the mountains. An hour's drive from Limassol or 90 minutes from Nicosia, its hotels, shops and restaurants (serving delicious locally caught trout) make Pano Platres a good starting point for exploring the surrounding forests. In the summer, regional folk arts are celebrated with a craftwork fair and a festival of music and theatre.

Caledonian Falls
The waters of the Kryos Potamos river cascade some 15 m (50 ft) over a steep precipice just 30 minutes' walk from Platres. On the way, you pass the Psilon Dhendron trout farm. From the Caledonian Falls, you can follow, in reverse order of its numbered signposts, a nature trail laid out along the river by the Forestry Department. But if you prefer your hikes to go downhill, start out from the trail's beginning at the Presidential Residence near the town of Troodos. An illustrated booklet (free from Platres' tourist information office) details the region's flowers, shrubs and trees signposted along the trail—among them, wild plum trees, black poplar, golden oak and Calabrian pine, Cyprus crocus, dog rose and myrtle.

Phini

A typical mountain village west of Platres, Phini has a funny little folklore museum, a friendly café and a traditional family-run pottery much appreciated for its handsome red ceramics. At the workshop, you can buy or just watch.

Troodhitissa Monastery

The present sanctuary northwest of Pano Platres was built in the 18th century, after forest fires had twice destroyed previous shrines. Two hermits are said to have built the original refuge here in 1250 after discovering an ancient icon of the Virgin Mary and Child in a nearby cave. Many a prudent fiancée and childless wife make a pilgrimage to the monastery, especially on Assumption Day (August 15). They come to pray to the revered icon and invoke fertility powers attributed to a sacred leather belt which monks happily tie around their waist.

Troodos Town

Ten kilometres (6 miles) up the mountain from Pano Platres, this lively little town is very popular with young people from Limassol or Nicosia at the weekend, but much quieter on weekdays. At 1,676 m (5,500 ft), it is the highest resort on the island. In summer, it offers tennis and well-organized rambling, and from January to March, some respectable skiing with four ski-lifts serving its two main pistes.

Besides the Caledonian Falls mentioned above, the Forestry Department has laid out three other nature trails around Troodos, each beginning in or near the town. Varying in length from 3 km (just less than 2 miles) to 9 km (5 miles), they take you past craggy ravines through fascinating forests of black pine standing out starkly against the russet-coloured soil. If all that sounds too strenuous, a nicely asphalted road takes vehicles to the peak of Mount Olympus. Turn your back on the ugly military radar station, and behold the whole island from its highest point, 1,951 m (6,401 ft).

An excursion northwest of Mount Olympus leads through enchanting countryside to Kykko, the island's most famous monastery. Orchards, almond and walnut groves alternate with vineyards and pine forests. Ramblers will find overnight accommodation and decent restaurants at Prodhromos.

Pedhoulas

In spring, the region is sweet with the fragrance of apple and pear blossom, but the most spectacular display is the pink cherry blossom down at Pedhoulas. 47

Grapes as big as figs, ripe for the wine vat, plucked on the southern slopes of the Troodos Mountains.

Visit the smaller of the town's two churches, that of Archangel Michael, portrayed quite ferociously in one of the frescoes inside. The monumental cedar in the centre of the village is said, not by legend but by the authoritative Forestry Department, to be nearly 500 years old.

Kykko

About 20 km (12 miles) west of Pedhoulas, in the depths of a mighty forest of pine and oak, Kykko Monastery stands aloof from the outside world but attracts the island's greatest crowds of pilgrims. It is here that Archbishop Makarios served as a novice and is now buried. But long before that, the 900-year-old foundation derived its fame from an icon of the Virgin Mary said to have been painted by St Luke. Endowed with miraculous rain-making powers, the silver-gilt icon has emerged unscathed from numerous forest fires and is naturally enough the object of particular veneration by fruit farmers and market gardeners.

The wealthy monastery has built gleaming new premises to receive the hundreds of pilgrims who come here for blessings and baptisms. Their votive offerings piled around the icon under the monks' grateful, watchful eyes include everything from jewellery and cash to simple wax figurines. There is a delightful café terrace overlooking the surrounding hills. On a hill above the monastery is the tomb of Archbishop Makarios in the form of a hermit's cave, with an honour guard of the Cypriot army.

Cedar Valley

The beautiful grove of cedar trees rises from a forest of plane, gold oak and Aleppo pines some 14 km (9 miles) west of Kykko. It's a bumpy road but well worth the trip, a perfect place for a picnic. The Forestry Department says there are about 50,000 of these noble trees here. The oldest, about 30 m (100 ft) tall, dates back to the time of the Crusades, nearly 900 years ago. The trees are said to be very resistant to modern air pollution.

Kakopetria

Improved roads have made this attractive hill resort north of Troodos town as easy to reach from Nicosia as from Limassol. Either way, the trip is rewarded by one of the most handsome old towns on the island. Splendid balconied houses have been restored to preserve the fine masonry of multi-hued local stone. They are built along a leafy ravine overlooking an old

---

BACKACHE? SEE ESAIAS

When it comes to founding a monastery, raising from the dead is a pretty good miracle, but curing chronic backache is not bad either. In 1094, after the great and good monk Esaias rid the Governor of Cyprus of his sciatica, he was sent to Constantinople to cure the daughter of Emperor Alexius Comnenus of the same problem. In exchange, Esaias brought back to Cyprus the hallowed icon attributed to St Luke and a rich land endowment for Kykko.

---

wooden flour mill. Plan lunch or dinner here to try the local trout. A few minutes' drive southwest of Kakopetria, the picturesque monastery church of St Nicholas of the Roof *(Ayios Nikolaos tis Steyis)* derives its strange name from its double roof: the original domed, tiled roof was covered with shingles in the 13th century. But the church is also worth visiting for its frescoes, the oldest painted at the time of its foundation in the 11th century. Later frescoes, from the 14th century, depict Jesus' life leading up to the Crucifixion. Three other "painted churches" can be visited at Galata, just to the north of Kakopetria.

NORTHERN CYPRUS
Northern Nicosia, Kyrenia, Famagusta

In sheer practical terms, it is just not possible (at the time of publication) to visit Turkish-occupied northern Cyprus with the same ease and thoroughness as the rest of the island. The only border crossing is in Nicosia, on Marcos Drakos Avenue next to what was the Ledra Palace Hotel. The crossing opens at 8 a.m. with obligatory same-day return at nightfall, latest 6 p.m. Sign in with your passport number at the Greek-Cypriot checkpoint. You cannot take a rental car across, but Turkish-Cypriot taxis, shared or individual service, are stationed at the Turkish checkpoint. You will have to pay a small fee for a one-day visa. You can buy Turkish lira for meals and other incidental costs, but Greek-Cypriot money will be accepted. Conditions change in this militarily sensitive region, but the taxi driver will know what is out of bounds to visitors or forbidden for photography.

Northern Nicosia

The main entrance to this community of 41,000 people is through the Kyrenia Gate, near the Turkish Embassy, the only diplomatic representation that recognizes Turkish-Cypriot sovereignty. On Kyrenia Avenue, the multi-domed 17th-century Mevlevi Tekke, once the mosque of the whirling dervish sect, is now a museum of Turkish-Cypriot folk art, notable for its musical instruments and costumes.

Ataturk Square, centre of Turkish-Cypriot business life, is dominated by an ancient Greek column from Salamis brought here by the Venetians. Their Lion of St Mark has long gone, replaced today by a modern copper globe.

Two Turkish Inns

On Asmaalti Street are two monumental *caravanserai* dating back to the 17th century. The two-storey Büyük Khan ("Great Inn"), slated to become a museum, has 68 rooms around an inner courtyard, with a small prayer-mosque in the centre. Kumarcilar Khan ("Gamblers' Inn"), now housing the Turkish-Cypriot archaeological institute, is of similar design.

Selimiye Mosque

Minarets on what was once the 14th-century French Gothic cathedral of St Sophia mark the Turkish conquest of 1570.

Previously, it had been the church of Latin (Catholic) Christian worship, where the Lusignan kings were crowned. Statues of saints, kings and church fathers still grace the pointed arches of the western façade, characteristically French in its portals and rose window. In the now whitewashed interior, pulpit and altar have been replaced by their Islamic *minbar* and *mihrab* counterparts.

Bedestan

The nearby Gothic structure was transformed from two adjacent churches, first to store grain, then as a cloth market and now disused. Notice the statue of St Nicholas and Venetian coats of arms sculpted in stone above the Gothic portals.

A street market extends down towards the Green Line border.

Kyrenia

Guarded by a formidable castle, Kyrenia (Girne in Turkish), population 7,600, can justly claim to possess one of the Mediterranean's prettiest natural harbours. In a town without the hectic crowds of the south coast resorts, the great attraction for a day trip is seafood lunch at a portside restaurant.

Up above the west side of the harbour, the 19th-century Ayios Archangelos Church houses a collection of icons rescued from other churches in the Turkish-occupied region.

Castle

First built to defend the Byzantine fleet against Arab raids in the 7th century, the fortress was subsequently expanded by the Crusaders, Venetians and Turks. It has long served as a prison for political enemies, including those of the British prior to independence in 1960. Sadik Pasha, Kyrenia's Turkish conqueror in 1570, is entombed in the entrance corridor. Beyond, you can visit the Byzantine chapel and the rulers' living quarters.

In the guardroom, a Shipwreck Museum shelters a Greek merchant vessel of the 4th century BC, one of the oldest wrecks ever recovered, with its cargo, from the seabed. It was discovered just north of Kyrenia harbour in 1965. Still preserved are oil jugs, wine jars from Rhodes and jars of almonds.

Bellapais Abbey

Completed in the 14th century, the Augustinian abbey stands in lovely ruin up in the hills overlooking Kyrenia and the sea. Destruction has been ecumenical: the monastery was plundered by good Genoese Catholics long before Turkish invaders took 51 their share, followed by the British Army pouring in cement for a military hospital. Nature is kinder: cypress, olive, orange and palm trees enhance the charm of the cloister's Gothic arcade, also adorned by stone carvings of animals real and mythical. In the handsomely vaulted refectory, with its fine rose window, you can see traces of the monks' wooden benches along the walls.

Crusaders' Castles

Three Gothic strongholds of the Crusaders straddle the jagged ridge of the Kyrenia Mountains. (Because of their strategic positions, some are used by the Turkish Army for training and may be out of bounds.)

St Hilarion Castle is usually open, its three tiers of towers and battlements clinging to a mountain peak. The castle erected by the French Lusignans on what was originally a Byzantine monastery was, like the others, deliberately left to ruin by the Venetians. It's a steep but manageable climb to the top, altitude 670 m (2,197 ft), and the view is magnificent.

True to its name, Buffavento, now just a noble pile of rubble, withstood buffeting winds to guard the direct route between the north coast and Nicosia. At 954 m (3,129 ft), its inaccessibility made it more useful as a prison than an active fortress. The reward for a rather strenuous climb up the mountain path is a view that will take away any breath you have left.

At the east end of the range surrounded by forests and olive groves, Kantara castle was, like St Hilarion, expanded from a Byzantine structure to guard the Karpas peninsula.

Famagusta

It began as a port of call for Christian pilgrims heading to and from Palestine and then enjoyed a flamboyant heyday under Genoese and Venetian merchants. Stagnating under the Ottoman Empire, Famagusta (Gazimagusa to the Turks), population 21,000, flourished again in the 20th century as Cyprus's main port and bustling tourist town. The second Turkish occupation, of 1974, caused another slump after the Greek-Cypriot community was expelled from the southern beach resort district of Varosha (now out of bounds). The city's historic monuments have survived and make the town worth a short visit.

Venetian Fortifications

The ramparts failed to stop the Turks in 1571, but the moated Tower of Othello, with a turret at each corner, still stands down

When Salamis was the island's capital, the Romans exercised mind and body in the Gymnasium.

by the harbour. Shakespeare is thought to have modelled his tragic hero on Cristoforo Moro, black Lieutenant Governor of the island in the 16th century. The Venetian Lion of St Mark is carved over the citadel's barrel-arched entrance.

Over on the northwest corner of the town's historic centre, the mighty Martinengo Bastion did prove too tough for the Turks, and its walls, up to 6 m (19 ft) thick, were left intact.

Lala Mustafa Pasha Mosque

One slender minaret distinguishes the town's most imposing Islamic shrine, otherwise better known to admirers of French Gothic as St Nicholas Cathedral, consecrated in 1326. Renamed after Famagusta's conqueror, the mosque has been stripped of its Christian iconography—frescoes, stained-glass windows and statuary. But the finely carved architectural detail of the porches and rose window on its western façade remind us it was once the most handsome church on the island.

Venetian Governor's Palace

Near the mosque, the Renaissance residence makes use of four ancient Doric columns transported from nearby Salamis 53 for the three arches of its façade. Left to decay, the palace ended up rather ignominiously as a prison in the 19th century.

Salamis

Excavated some 9 km (5 miles) north of Famagusta, this was the most powerful of the island's city kingdoms in classical Greek antiquity. Exiled artists and writers flocked here from Athens, and its population numbered 100,000 in its heyday. Salamis became the Christian capital of Cyprus. Damaged by numerous earthquakes, it disappeared only with the Arab conquest of 649. Among the late Greek, Roman and Byzantine vestiges that have survived, the most striking is the Roman theatre seating 15,000 spectators. Closer to the sea is the Gymnasium (public school), rendered more elegant by Corinthian columns which the Byzantines transferred here from the theatre. Next to the school are the Public Baths, complete with cold, tepid and hot room.

St Barnabas Monastery

Just west of Salamis, an 18th-century monastery church stands near the grave of Barnabas, who accompanied Paul on his mission to Cyprus in AD 45. It was here, buried beneath a carob tree, that a manuscript of Matthew's gospel was found and presented to the Byzantine emperor in exchange for church autonomy in Cyprus. The drum-domed church has been built with pillars, capitals and other masonry from ancient Salamis.

THE SIX BEST TURKISH-CYPRIOT LANDMARKS In the short time available for a first visit to Northern Cyprus, you may want to know the sightseeing "musts". In northern Nicosia, the **Selimiye Mosque** converted from a Gothic Cathedral; **Kyrenia Harbour**, maritime jewel of the Mediterranean; **Bellapais Abbey**, enchantingly situated medieval Augustinian ruin; **St Hilarion Castle**, Crusaders' redoubt in the Kyrenia Mountains; **Famagusta's Venetian fortifications**, including the famous Tower of Othello; **Salamis**, ancient Greek city kingdom with Roman theatre and Gymnasium.

Shopping

An unexpected positive fallout of the island's 1974 partition has been the renewal of traditional Cypriot craftwork. Many Greek-Cypriot refugees from rural areas in the north have found employment in the south as artisans reviving the talents of their ancestors in ceramics, copperware, woodcarving and weaving. Many of them work for the non-profit Cyprus Handicraft Service (CHS). Their shops in Nicosia, Paphos, Limassol and Larnaca give you a good idea of the range of goods available, often of more reliable quality and authenticity than in the more commercial souvenir shops. But you will of course also find the genuine article in mountain villages, with the bonus of watching it being made.

Carpets

The Turkish influence is apparent in brightly coloured Oriental patterns, both for floor coverings and wall hangings. You will also find thick Greek-style woollen rugs.

Ceramics

Vases and fruit dishes reproduce ancient Cypriot styles in their glazed geometric patterns. The rural tradition continues unbroken in robust oil jars and wine jugs. Look out, too, for nicely reproduced terracotta statuettes of animals and the pagan gods of antiquity. Potters in Phini produce distinctive red earthenware.

Copper and Brass

The industry that gave the island its name continues in handcrafted copper pots and kitchen utensils. Similar skills are applied to brass candlesticks and trays.

Embroidery and Textiles

Embroidered linen is without a doubt the most successful of Cyprus's cottage industries. In all the major resorts you will find beautifully finished goods, from handkerchiefs and doilies to tablecloths and pillow cases. The finest work is known as *lefkaritika*, on sale all over the island, but best of all in its home town of

An Orthodox priest continues the time-honoured art of icon-painting.

Lefkara. Elsewhere, hand-woven fabrics can be bought to be tailored on the spot. If you feel like thinking of colder weather back home, the local heavy woollen sweaters are a fair bargain.

Gourmet Gifts

Take home a clay pot of the tangy local olives, a box of Turkish Delight (whoops! *loukoumia*), best from Lefkara or Yeroskipos, and a bottle or two of Aphrodite white or Commandaria sweet red dessert wine.

Jewellery

Silver and gold (usually 18-karat) are a speciality, often reproducing the intricate filigree patterns of Byzantine tradition.

Leatherware

Styling in leather clothing is at best rustic, more attractive for sandals and shoes than for jackets and tunics. The robust local hides are ideal for bags, satchels and belts.

Woodcarving

You may just want to settle for a finely carved picture frame or tea tray, but the Cyprus Handicraft Service can also arrange to ship one of those splendid bridal dowry chests displayed in every folklore museum on the island.

Dining Out

Cypriot cuisine makes a happy marriage of its Greek and Turkish origins. Its savoury variety offers a welcome change from the too often bland "international" cuisine of the hotel's set menu. The meat, whether beef, pork, lamb or goat, is served in generous portions. Fish-lovers have a good choice of seafood and freshwater fish from the mountain rivers. And the island's flourishing agriculture guarantees that you get plenty of fresh vegetables and salads. For local colour, seek out tavernas away from the seafront and dine a little later— 9 to 10 p.m. Some of the best tavernas have no written menu at all, just a fixed-price dinner where you can be sure of a good traditional meal. In any case, nobody leaves Cyprus hungry.

To Start With...

For some, the endless array of starters known here as *mezedhes* is a meal in itself. To save room for a main dish, Cypriots sample, but do not finish off, every delicacy placed before them. You can either choose among the dozens of different little dishes available or, if you're a novice, let the waiter bring an assortment of five or six. The parade usually begins with olives, black and green, plain or dressed in lemon, garlic, coriander or peppers. Then come the dips—*tahini* (sesame seed paste), *houmous* (chickpea purée), *taramosalata* (smoked cod roe), *melidzano*

(aubergine) or *dzadziki* (yoghurt and cucumber, with mint or garlic). The stuffed vine leaves are called *dolmades* and pickled cauliflower *moungra*. Eat these with the delicious *koulouria* (sesame bread), *elioti* (olive bread) or flat unleavened *pita*.

The jumbo *choriatiki salata*— white cabbage, lettuce, tomatoes, cucumber, fresh coriander, capers, onions and *feta* cheese, is a meal in itself.

Top of the cold seafood list come *kalamari* (squid) and *oktapodhi ksidhato* (thinly sliced octopus), but you might like to try the *karaoli yachni* (snails in tomato sauce).

The hors d'œuvres may also include little sausages made from pork, lamb or veal—smoked *sheftalia* or *loukanika*.

Two soups: *avgolemono* (egg and lemon) and the hearty *trahanas* of cracked wheat and yoghurt.

Main Course: Fish or Meat?

If you can still manage it, the most common fish dishes, baked, grilled or sautéed, are red mullet (*barbounia*), sea bass (*sinagrida*), swordfish (*xifias*) or deep fried whitebait (*marida*). In the Troodos mountain resorts, ask for freshwater trout (*pestrophes*). Shellfish are more likely to be frozen—spiny lobster, shrimp and squid.

Beef or veal stew (*stifado*) is the most robust of the meat dishes. The pork equivalent, with red wine and coriander, is known as *afelia*. Another favourite pork dish is charcoal-grilled suckling pig. Besides kebabs (*souvlakia*) and chops, lamb or mutton is delicious barbecued (*kleftiko*), baked in a clay pot with greens and beans (*louvia me lahana*), or as spicy meat balls (*keftedes*).

Moussaka is also popular—layers of minced beef, aubergine, zucchini and spices with a cheese topping. Clearly influenced by the Venetians and Genoese, Cypriots like good pasta, both cheese-filled ravioli and tagliatelli in meat, tomato and cheese sauces.

Desserts

Local fresh fruit is too good to refuse: figs, pomegranates, apricots, peaches, cherries, plums, grapes. The ice cream is usually delicious and the Turkish-style pastries are heavenly: *baklava,* flaky pastry stuffed with honey and nuts; shredded *kataïfi; loukoumades,* doughnuts in syrup and *daktyla,* almond pastry.

Drinks

The beer, locally brewed with international labels, is fine and the wines are more than respectable. Among the commonest good dry whites are Aphrodite, Arsinoë, Bella Pais and Nefeli. More refined—but more difficult to find—is the Ayios Amvrosios produced by the Chrysorroyiatissa monastery, near Paphos. Best known of the reds is Othello, but try, too, Olympus Claret and Afames.

As an apéritif or dessert wine, the celebrated sweet red Commandaria will give you an idea of what the knights of old used to drink in their castle at Kolossi, near Limassol. Anise-flavoured *ouzo* makes a refreshing apéritif and for after dinner, try a snifter of Five Kings Cypriot brandy or Filfar liqueur.

Sports

Water Sports
For family swimming away from the hotel pool, try the sandy beaches of Ayia Napa, Fig Tree Bay and Protaras at the east end of the island or Coral Bay near Paphos at the west end. For a more secluded swim, head for the coves on the north coast's Chrysochou Bay or down around Cape Greco.

All the major resorts now provide equipment and instruction for serious scuba-diving and snorkelling. Amenities are also available for water-skiing, windsurfing, parasailing, canoeing and yachting.

Fishing
Hire a boat at any of the resort harbours to go out for the sea bream, mullet or swordfish and have your hotel prepare your catch for supper. Freshwater angling requires a licence from the Fisheries Department—details from the tourist information office.

Rambling and Cycling
Nobody needs flinch from the nature trails in the Troodos Mountains or above the cliffs of the Akamas peninsula. The tourist offices provide detailed trail-maps. To really stretch your legs, hire a mountain bike from Paphos or Troodos town. For something less strenuous, stroll or cycle across the mudflats on Akrotiri peninsula or the Salt Lake near Larnaca and try a little quiet birdwatching.

Tennis
The bigger hotels have good asphalt or clay courts, but bring your own racquet. In summer, enthusiasts head for the cooler public courts up at Troodos.

Skiing
Yes, skiing. Besides several cross-country trails through the forests, Troodos operates four ski-lifts from January to March for two quite honourable pistes on Mount Olympus.

Spectator Sports
From September to June, weekend horse racing draws punters to the Nicosia racecourse at Ayio Dhometios. The three-day international Cyprus Car Rally takes place in September around the Troodos mountain roads.

The Hard Facts

Airports

International flights come into Larnaca or Paphos. Larnaca Airport is 6 km (3 miles) from town, 50 km (30 miles) from Nicosia. The terminal provides banking, car-hire and tourist information office services. The smaller Paphos airport, with just currency exchange, duty-free and restaurant facilities, is 11 km (7 miles) from the resort.

Climate

Cyprus enjoys the most attractive of Mediterranean climates, plenty of sun—340 days a year at the coast—without uncomfortable humidity. Even in the heat of high summer, you can always find relief in coastal breezes or escape for a while to the cool of the Troodos and Kyrenia mountains. In July and August, temperatures average 29°C (85°F), but in the other summer months you will find a more bearable 27°C (80°F). The most pleasant surprise is the mellow autumn and winter, occasional rain from October to early March, but lots of sun, too. Up in the Troodos mountains, it snows enough in January and February for skiing.

Communications

To get your holiday postcards back home before you do, disguise them as letters inside envelopes and the post office will treat them more seriously. Hotel fax and telephone services are remarkably good, but be patient in high season. Although the post office is cheaper, you may feel it worth paying the hotel surcharge to avoid waiting in line and having to depend on opening hours.

Crime

Most Cypriots are very honest. Pickpockets are much commoner elsewhere in Europe, but without undue paranoia, don't tempt the few that do exist anywhere with an open handbag or a wallet in the hip pocket. Leave your valuables in the hotel safe. Lock your luggage before leaving it with porters at the airport.

Currency

The Cyprus pound (CY£) is divided into 100 cents, with coins ranging from 1 to 50 cents and banknotes from CY£ 1 to 20.

Increasingly, shops and restaurants welcome credit cards

and often prefer them to cash. Eurocheques are accepted, but traveller's cheques must be cashed at a bank or hotel.

Driving

If you are renting a car, be sure to have a valid national licence or International Driving Permit. Minimum age for rental is usually 21, sometimes 25. Speed limits are 50 kph in town, 80 kph on roads and 100 kph on the motorway. As in Britain, drive on the left, overtake on the right. The motorway (expressway) network linking Nicosia, Limassol and Larnaca is first class. There are good secondary roads and a fair amount of bumpy mountain roads. Cypriot drivers drive with zippy Mediterranean temperament, but are generally more disciplined than Greeks and Turks.

Electric Current

Britain has bequeathed its three-pin plugs and sockets on 220/240 volts AC, 50 Hz. But most hotel bathrooms have two-pin outlets for 220/110-volt razors.

Emergencies

Most problems can be handled at your hotel desk. One telephone number for police, fire or ambulance: **199.** Your consulate is there only for critical situations, lost passports or worse, but not lost cash or plane tickets.

Entry Formalities

A valid passport is all most people need, but make sure it does not have a stamp in it from northern Cyprus. People coming in from the Turkish-controlled ports of Kyrenia, Famagusta or Karavostasi or the northern airport of Ercan cannot cross into the Greek-Cypriot republic.

Customs controls are minimal at point of entry, with an official import or export allowance of 200 cigarettes or 50 cigars or 250 g of tobacco, 1 bottle wine and 1 litre spirits. No limit on amounts of foreign currency, but you must declare amounts over US$1,000. Any amounts imported in local currency must be declared on arrival.

Essentials

Pack very little. Clothing should be light—cottons are less sticky than synthetics. You won't need much formal wear. Pack a foldable sun hat and add a sweater for cool evenings. Good walking-shoes are vital, as well as easy-to-kick-off sandals or moccasins for mosques. Include insect-repellent and a pocket torch—invaluable for dark Byzantine churches and beach barbecues.

Health

The island's good climate means there are no special health problems. As everywhere these days, 61 avoid excessive direct exposure to the sun. Wear a hat, use a sun screen, and keep to the shady side of the street when sightseeing. It's perfectly safe to drink the tap water. For emergencies, make sure your health insurance covers holiday illnesses as Cyprus's social security does not extend to foreign visitors. Doctors, dentists and hospital staff are of very high standard, many speaking good English. If you anticipate need of prescription medicines, take your own as you may not find the exact equivalent on the spot.

Languages

English and German are the most commonly spoken languages after Greek. Street signs are most often written in Greek and English. Spelling varies; you'll see Agios and Ayios, Agia and Ayia, Paphos and Pafos, Germasogeia and Yermasoyia. Never mind. It's all Greek to the locals.

Media

European newspapers and international editions of American papers are readily available.

Increasingly, hotels have satellite dishes for BBC World Service, CNN, German, French, Spanish and Italian television channels.

Besides island-wide access to BBC World Service radio, BFBS (British Forces Broadcasting Service) radio is beamed around the "Sovereign Base Areas" near Limassol and Larnaca.

Opening Hours

The following times are always subject to variations.

Banks open 8.15 a.m. to 12.30 p.m. for normal business, but often again from 4 to 6 p.m. for currency exchange.

Shops are open in summer 8 a.m. to 1 p.m. and again from 4 to 7 p.m. From October to April, afternoon opening is from 2.30 to 5.30 p.m. They close Wednesday and Saturday afternoons, and all day Sunday.

Most museums open early on the coast, 7.30 or 8 a.m. and an hour later in Nicosia and nearly all stay open in the lunch hour. Most close Saturday afternoon and Sunday, but as a rule closing times vary greatly, so check first with the local tourist information office.

Photography

Film for video or still cameras is available. If you buy supplies ahead of time, choose film speeds suitable for the brilliant Mediterranean light. Most museums allow cameras, but you should ask permission. Photography is forbidden around military installations and in the vicinity of the border with Turkish-occupied northern Cyprus.

Public Holidays

Cyprus's public holidays are both historical (some shared with Greece) and religious:

January 1	New Year
January 6	Epiphany
March 25	Greek Independence Day
April 1	Cyprus Struggle Day
May 1	Labour Day
August 15	Assumption Day
October 1	Cyprus Independence Day
October 28	"No" Day, commemorating Greek resistance to Italian invasion in 1940
December 25	Christmas Day
December 26	Boxing Day

Moveable holidays are the first day of Lent, Good Friday, Easter Monday and Whitsuntide.

Public Transport

It's simple. There are no trains and few buses. Taxis, individual or shared, are efficient, honest and reasonable in price.

Social Graces

Contact with ordinary Cypriots is much easier than you might imagine. In the towns, many speak a few words of English, but a handshake and a couple of words of Greek from you—*parakalo,* please, or *efcharisto,* thank you—can work wonders in getting a friendly response, especially if you smile. Remember that when you enter a church, modest dress is essential—no shorts or bare shoulders—and in a mosque, take off your shoes. Keep your swimwear for the beach or swimming pool.

Tipping

Gratuities are based on the European rather than Middle Eastern model, with service charges included in hotel and restaurant bills. Add a little when the service has been particularly good. Taxi drivers and tour guides should be tipped around 10 per cent; hairdressers 10 to 15 per cent.

Toilets

In general, they are good and hygienic, noticeably on public beaches. If you cannot find a public toilet in town and prefer to use the facilities of a café or restaurant, you should order at least a coffee.

Tourist Information Offices

The Cyprus Tourism Organisation (CTO) has information offices in the main resorts. They are extremely helpful and well organized, and provide superb street plans and maps of nature trails, brochures. They also have up-to-date information on the ever-changing opening hours.

INDEX

General editor: Barbara Ender-Jones
Photos: B. Joliat, P. Ducommun, C. Hervé-Bazin, Y. Leuba
Design: Dominique Michellod, Corsier/Vevey
Maps: JPM Publications

Copyright ©1999, 1995 by JPM Publications SA
12 avenue William-Fraisse, 1006 Lausanne, Switzerland
E-mail: information@jpmguides.com
Web site: http://www.jpmguides.com/

Printed in Switzerland—Gessler/Sion
Edition 1999–2000